D1196981

living style

de-stress

acknowledgements

I would like to thank Catie Ziller, Anne Wilson, Matt Handbury and Jackie Frank for their ongoing support and the opportunity to develop this series. Thank you to everyone at Murdoch Books and Merehurst Publishing who has been involved in this project for their continuous hard work. I would also like to say a big thank you to photographer Chris Craymer for his inspiration, endless enthusiasm and creativity and for capturing the spirit of this book on film. Thank you to Martyn Gayle and Attracta Courtney for their hard work and fab hair and make-up. Special thanks to Susie for all her hard work and great organising for the shoot production.

Most of all I would like to thank those closet to me, Danny, Susie, Stewart and Lottie, who supported me from start to finish, especially when the going got tough; to my mum Brenda for her inspiration, to my dad Brian for his constant drive and to my grandma for her worldly advice. Thank you to Nicola, Sam and Michael, who kept me smiling. I couldn't have got this far without you all.

Special thanks to the Tuckers for the loan of the wellies, Sam Girdwood, all the models who appeared in the book, Emi, Nancy Brady and the team at NBPR, and Lavish Locations. Thank you for the loan of the following items for photography: Liza Bruce swimwear (pp. 68, 74, 77), tel 44 20 7235 8423; Muji underwear (pp. 16, 25, 42, 48, 51, 56, 63, 66), tel 44 20 7221 9360; Cath Kidson shower cap (p. 64), tel 44 20 7221 4000; Sean Arnold Sporting Antiques, tel 44 20 7221 2267; hair extensions by Trendco, tel 44 20 7221 2646; Space Boudoir pashmina (p. 78), www.boudoir@spaceshop.co.uk

living style

de-stress

jane campsie

photography by chris craymer

TIME
LIFE
BOOKS

contents

anxiety

stress

tension

under pressure

chaos

agitation

frustration

feeling stressed-out

Stress has been described as the disease of modern society: We can't live with it, we can't live without it. When we are under too much pressure we tend to live our lives on over-drive and on the verge of burnout, whereas when there is insufficient stress in our lives we can be faced with boredom and the frustrations of not having enough stimulation. So how do we strike the right balance? The problem is not how much stress we are under, but how we cope and adapt to stress. We all react to different levels and types of stress in various ways. When under pressure, the body releases hormones—mainly adrenaline and cortisol—that raise blood pressure and create that familiar heart-pounding sensation. At the same time, the blood flow to the digestive system is reduced and the blood supply to the muscles is increased. This commonly leads to feelings of nausea and "butterflies in the stomach." Adrenaline also stimulates the release of glucose and essential fatty acids into the bloodstream to refuel the muscles and maximize our reflexes. While our blood and heart pressure increase, our breathing becomes shallower. When the stressful situation has passed, our body returns to normal. However, long-term stress takes its toll, making it harder for the body to bounce back.

strike a balance

survival tactics

The body reacts to stress with a "fight or flight" response. In most situations today, this primeval reaction to a threat or challenge is not considered socially acceptable. Now, when the pressure is on, we have to find other ways to deal with the stressful situation.

stress damage

Our tolerance levels to controlling our physical and emotional response to stress vary. When stress levels are high, our mind, body, emotions, and behavior are affected. Common symptoms include headaches, backaches, nervous twitches, tooth-grinding, and sleep disorders. Over prolonged periods, stress manifests itself in more serious disorders, such as high blood pressure, digestive problems, diabetes, insomnia, fatigue, and stomach ulcers. On an emotional level, stress can cause mood swings, depression, irritability, and lack of concentration.

positive effects

Since the stresses and strains of modern living are here to stay, it is vital that we adopt a positive attitude and see how we can make stress work to our advantage. Stress can, in fact, have a positive effect on how we feel and behave, provided we don't allow our stress levels to rise too high. Minor stress can present a challenge and an opportunity to perform to the best of our ability. When we are under pressure our energy levels are usually higher, enabling us to function at our optimum. Stress can also act as a form of motivation. Furthermore, once we have completed a stressful task, the sense of achievement we feel is a healthy boost to our self-esteem. There is also the reward at the end—our relaxation time—and our appreciation of this is heightened after the stressful situation has passed. The secret is to learn how much stress you can live with, without letting it become a destructive force.

life stressors

physical stress

Unnecessary pressure on the body leads to physical complaints such as strained muscles, aches and pains, and, at worst, diseases such as arthritis and diabetes. The best way to overcome physical stress is to exercise regularly, look at your posture, find the most comfortable way to sit at a desk or computer, do regular stretching movements, and learn to gauge what your body can safely endure.

emotional stress

Stress can affect the mind as powerfully as the body. We can become irritable, over-sensitive, argumentative, spiteful, or withdrawn. Long-term emotional stress can lead to anxiety-related disorders and depression, and can put stress on relationships. Combat emotional stress by talking about problems, putting things in perspective, and working at relationships. Emotional stress caused by bereavement or separation requires support, love, and understanding.

environmental stress

Environmental stress is triggered by factors in the home, workplace, or community. The most common include pollution, noise, overcrowding, and untidiness. First address the stresses that can be dealt with most easily. For example, if you get anxious sitting in traffic jams, consider other means of travel. Work-related stresses such as deadlines and work overload should be discussed with colleagues and solved.

burnout

When stresses build up over a long period of time we suffer burnout. This is identified by feelings of fatigue and a lack of motivation. Burnout often occurs when we try to achieve too much in too short a space of time, or when we do not prioritize our time and consequently have to overstretch ourselves. The best solution is to take a break, go on vacation (even a few days can help), and learn effective stress-management techniques.

release it

ON THE average, adults laugh 15 times a day, compared with children, who laugh roughly 400 times a day.

89 PERCENT of adults say that they experience high stress levels.

THE HIGHEST stress ratings, in descending order of severity, are caused by: death of one's partner, marital breakdown, a pending prison sentence, death of a close relative, personal injury or illness, getting married, losing a job, and moving.

STRESS-RELATED problems, such as migraines and headaches, are responsible for high rates of employee absenteeism in Western countries.

MORE PEOPLE suffer heart attacks at 9 o'clock on Monday morning than at any other time of the week.

75 TO 90 percent of visits to doctors by adults are for stress-related problems.

ONE IN four people suffer sleep deprivation as a result of stress, and research has shown that women are more likely to suffer from stress-related sleeping disorders than men. Sufferers of emotional stress or grief need more sleep than unstressed people.

70 TO 80 percent of all disease and illness is stress related. Common conditions include insomnia, headaches, colds, migraines, and heart disease.

control

organize

overcome

stress management

balance

achieve

adapt

how can you manage stress?

The secrets to effective stress management lie in controlling the way in which you react to stress and in gauging the safe level of stress under which you can function. The first step is to identify what causes you to feel stressed. Is it your work? Is it your home life? Are you setting yourself unrealistic goals, overstretching yourself, or taking on too much? Do you suffer from chronic lack of time? Once you have identified the problem, do something positive about combating it.

Short-term stress utilizes adrenaline and other hormones to maximize your performance, whereas long-term stress, which causes adrenaline levels to remain high and fatigue is a constant, will affect your performance. You cannot get away from the stresses of modern life, so you must make sure that your health is optimal so you can cope when the pressure is on. On an emotional level, try not to exaggerate your stressors— things aren't always as bad as they may seem. It is also essential to monitor how you react physically to stress and then attempt to improve things. Incorporate simple breathing exercises, relaxation techniques, exercise, and meditation into your daily routine so you can handle life when the going gets tough.

taking control

stressed-out

If you feel you cannot cope, have a tendency to snap easily, sleep badly, have a reduced sex drive, find it difficult to concentrate, eat when you are not hungry, often feel close to tears, have problems communicating with people, and think you have lost your sense of humor, the chances are you are suffering from stress.

stop worrying

Often we worry about things that are not going to happen or that are beyond our control. The main causes of unnecessary anxiety include wanting love and admiration, being afraid of not living up to peoples' expectations, not being in control of fate, and believing that bad experiences of the past will repeat themselves in the future.

balance it

There are simple steps you can take to boost your tolerance to stress. If you find your optimum stress level—that is, the degree at which you function most effectively when the pressure is on—you can use stress to your benefit. The best way to find your optimum stress level is to keep a diary for a number of weeks, outlining your highs and lows and how you felt on different days, depending on what pressure you were under. Use the days when you felt happy and in control (even if things were hectic and frantic) as a guide for gauging what level of stress suits you. Observe how much time you need for yourself, how much sleep you require, and look closely at your diet and exercise regimens. Then plan your life accordingly.

taking control

time management

It is important to use your time in the most productive way possible. Effective time management helps reduce work-related stress, ensuring that you are in control, productive, and have a life outside of work. Time management is also beneficial if you are trying to juggle the various pressures of a family, career, household duties, relationships, and a social life and want some time to yourself. Try to focus on the results, not the activity. Start off by analyzing how effectively you are currently using your time, prioritize your tasks, and see what you can delegate. Plan in advance and set yourself realistic deadlines and achievable goals. Avoid distractions and take regular breaks; you will function much better if you stop and refresh yourself.

setting guidelines

Discipline yourself to adopt a positive attitude. Criticizing others breeds negativity, so try to be a more positive person. Examine your good qualities and those of others. Learn to be more tolerant and to forgive others; holding grudges will only lead to awkward situations and cause anxiety. Also, avoid unnecessary competition, especially if you're a bad loser. Too many competitive situations can lead to tension and aggression. If you're a worrier, start talking about your troubles. Remember, a problem shared is a problem halved. Finally, make sure you have some fun and make time for yourself. Plan a vacation so you have something to look forward to. Most important of all, lighten up and live each day to the fullest.

get a grip

LEARN TO adapt to change and to increase your tolerance to stress.

MANAGE YOUR time wisely. Prioritize your daily schedule and always try to keep things in perspective.

GET THE facts. More often than not, we worry about problems without knowing all the facts. When we know the full story we often discover that there's nothing to worry about.

DON'T SET yourself unachievable goals or make demands on your time that are unrealistic.

TAKE TIME out to relax each day. Wallow in a warm bath, go for a walk, read a book, or listen to some music. Even when your schedule is hectic, make time for yourself.

DO YOUR best, but don't be hard on yourself if what you do isn't perfect.

SAY NO. You can't do everything, so free up some of your time to lighten your load when the pressure is on.

SHARE YOUR worries with a friend. Talking to people provides you with the assurance that you are not alone. Also, someone else's opinion or view can often put things in perspective.

DON'T DWELL on the past. Live in the present and don't worry about the future. Live each day as it comes.

DECIDE TO dispense with your worries. Too often we waste valuable time and energy worrying about things that are beyond our control. Channel these resources in a more constructive way.

peace

calm

tranquillity

living with stress

balance

control

serenity

organize your life

Let's face it, in an ideal world we would not have to lead a stressful lifestyle. But demands on our time, combined with emotional pressures and the difficulties of juggling a career, family, and relationships, mean that most of us cannot avoid the stresses of modern living. However, we *can* organize our life so we can deal with pressure and maintain balance and harmony, even when the going gets tough. It's not that hard. For starters, devise a routine to best organize the domestic chores in your life. If you are a born worrier, try making lists. Experts have proved that if you write down a list of your troubles or things you have to do, especially just before going to bed, it will help put a stop to unnecessary worry. Another way to get organized and stop feeling stressed is to limit the number of tasks you're going to undertake in one day. There are only a certain number of hours in the day; if you take on too much it will only interfere with your personal relaxation time and cut into your sleep time. A few final measures you can take to prevent chaos getting the upper hand are to make sure that your home environment is conducive to relaxation, that you get sufficient sleep, eat sensibly, and exercise daily.

stress-free environment

tidy up

Disorganization can breed stress, and mess and clutter are not conducive to an orderly mind. Unnecessary disorder will only make you feel that things are getting the best of you and that your life is chaotic. Keep your home and work environment in order, tidy up as you go and try to keep things organized.

fresh air

Air-conditioning, smoke, excess humidity or dryness, air pollution, and solvents from carpets and furniture will result in poor air quality. Improve conditions and reduce stress by ensuring that rooms are well ventilated. If possible, open the windows to get the air flowing freely. Surround yourself with plants; they will release oxygen into the environment and absorb carbon dioxide and pollutants. The more oxygen you get, the calmer you will be. Invest in a humidifier and place an ionizer near electrical equipment to eliminate the positive ions it creates.

lighten up

To illuminate a room, use daylight (either direct or filtered) wherever possible. Bad lighting, or lights that are too bright, can cause eyestrain, headaches, and fatigue. If illumination by natural means is not possible, invest in full-spectrum light bulbs that mimic natural daylight.

color schemes

Choose colors to suit your home or office and the mood you wish each room to reflect. Blue is relaxing and has the effect of lowering the heart rate and slowing respiration. Pink is also soothing: It relaxes the muscles, reduces anxiety, and encourages rest. Red, on the other hand, is stimulating. It increases the heart rate and steps up brain activity. Orange boosts the appetite and reduces fatigue, while yellow stimulates the memory, increases the pulse rate, and lifts the spirits. Green is an uplifting color: It relieves depression and soothes the mind and body.

stress-free environment

noise pollution

Noise can cause intense stress. Whether it's telephones ringing, people talking, machinery operating, music playing, children screaming, or just the general hum of background sound, high levels of noise can interfere with concentration. Our performance is affected and we feel agitated and annoyed. Look at ways to cut down on noise: In your home, install double-glazed windows, find quiet areas to retreat to for work and relaxation and, if all else fails, use earplugs.

personal space

It is essential to have your own space, both at work and at home. Keep one room, or one area of your home, as a relaxation area and use it to retreat to in times of stress. In this space, do not work, do household chores, or spend time on the phone; keep it solely as a place to relax and unwind. Keep the space cozy in winter and be sure a breeze can circulate in the summer.

good vibrations

Listening to soothing sounds will instantly calm the mind and body. Harmonious tunes prompt the brain to release a hormone, known as ACTH (adrenocorticotropic hormone), which has a calming effect on the body. Both humans and animals respond to music. Babies in the womb respond to music at four and a half months, and dogs and racehorses relax to certain harmonious tunes. To relax effectively, listen to sounds of the sea, rain forest, running water, or classical music.

ergonomic advice

Muscular tension can arise from uncomfortable furniture and the way in which you use it. If you spend long periods sitting at a desk, make sure you have the correct type of chair, one that offers sufficient support for the back. If you work at a computer for hours on end, make sure the keyboard and monitor are correctly positioned, and take breaks periodically.

sleep notions

nocturnal affairs

Experts recommend that we get 8 to 9 hours sleep each night. Although many people survive on fewer hours' sleep, what they probably don't realize is that insufficient sleep can interfere with concentration levels, limit our patience, make us less alert, and reduce the amount of energy we have. What's more, we are more likely to lose our sense of humor.

sleep disorders

One in four people suffers from a stress-related sleep disorder. These disorders fall into three categories: transient insomnia, which usually lasts from 3 to 4 days; short-term insomnia, which lasts from 7 to 14 days; and chronic insomnia, which lasts for 3 weeks or more. Whether you have an inability to fall asleep or stay asleep, sleeping pills are not the only solution. If relaxation and other techniques fail, herbs such as passiflora and valerian root offer safe alternatives.

culinary delights

If you have trouble sleeping, avoid drinking alcohol or caffeine for at least 2 hours before going to bed. A mug of warm milk at bedtime will help send you to sleep. Milk contains the amino acid tryptophan, a precursor to the calming brain chemical serotonin, which is important for relaxation. Also, milk is high in calcium, a mineral reputed to have muscle-relaxing benefits. Other foods that help induce sleep include bananas, figs, dates, yogurt, tuna, whole-grain crackers, and nuts. Avoid sugar, cheese, chocolate, potatoes, pork, spinach, and tomatoes at bedtime.

room conditions

Keep your bedroom well ventilated and comfortably cool. If the room is hot and stuffy you will wake up with something akin to a hangover. Be sure your room is dark when you go to bed. Avoid synthetic bed linen and place orchids or aloe vera—plants that produce more oxygen at night—in bedrooms.

get physical

regular exercise

The benefits of exercise are numerous: physical activity burns up calories, prevents diseases of the cardiovascular system, slows down the aging process, and keeps us trim and fit. Between 5 and 30 minutes of physical exercise daily is sufficient to relieve muscular strain, and can have a positive effect on mental clarity. For example, a brisk walk helps improve concentration and a bike ride can clear the mind. If you lead a stressful but sedentary lifestyle, make time to reap the benefits of physical exercise.

sporting choice

Look for an activity that will enhance your physical and mental well-being. Skipping, jogging, swimming, and walking are repetitive physical motions that take the mind off other concerns. Yoga improves flexibility and calms the mind and is a good activity for stressed-out people, as is t'ai chi, a form of moving meditation.

walking workout

Walking is beneficial for reducing stress and can actually enable your brain to function better. Studies have revealed that people who take a walk every day not only have stronger legs than nonwalkers but a larger number of brain cells. Try to go for a brisk walk every day, even if it is only for 10 or 15 minutes. Adapt your lifestyle to incorporate more walking. For example, take a walk instead of using the car or public transportation, and walk up and down stairs instead of using elevators and escalators.

intense activity

Forget gruelling workouts at the gym. If you are feeling stressed and you do a high-impact aerobics workout, the chances are you'll still be in overdrive afterward. Stress experts advise staying away from high-intensity activities and opting for low-impact sessions that will leave you feeling more relaxed and in control.

nutritional advice

healthy eating

When we are under pressure, the body uses up vital supplies of nutrients faster than usual, and we fluctuate between hyperactivity and a state of lethargy. Eat a diet rich in complex carbohydrates—fruits and vegetables, nuts, whole-grain cereal products—to fuel the body with a constant supply of energy. Such a diet will help calm the mind, increase stamina, and combat highs and lows. Don't skip breakfast: Eat a substantial meal of hot cereal or muesli to release energy slowly and steadily throughout the day. Opt for salad and vegetables with whole-wheat pasta, rice, or bread for lunch, and fresh fish, poultry, or meat and vegetables for dinner. Snack on fruits, nuts, and seeds. Avoid refined carbohydrates, including foods made from white flour—pasta, bread, cookies, cakes—and sugary foods. They give you a sudden surge of energy, but as your body reacts to stabilize high sugar levels it creates a slump in energy levels soon afterward.

food force

Eating small meals every 3 hours can help to sustain energy and vital vitamin levels. When we are stressed, B vitamins are depleted in an effort to keep the nervous system functioning properly, and vitamin C and zinc are used up fighting infection. Fresh fruits (especially citrus fruits) and vegetables supply your vitamin C needs, while zinc can be obtained from red meat, egg yolks, dairy produce, whole-grain cereals, and seafood. The B vitamins are found in many of the foods above, as well as in nuts, seeds, organ meats, and dried fruits.

prep work

Buy organic, fresh produce. Preserve or increase the nutritional content of food while preparing it: Don't salt water when cooking vegetables; tear, rather than chop, herbs and lettuce; always steam, poach, or grill foods; soak rice, legumes, and whole-grains overnight before cooking.

relaxed living

DRINK WATER—at least eight glasses a day—to help you cope when the pressure is on. A well-hydrated body will function more effectively.

TO RELAX, place some marbles in a large bowl and half-fill the bowl with warm water. Place your feet in it and run the soles of your feet over the marbles. The combination of this massage movement and the warm water works to dissipate aches and pains, providing instant relaxation.

YAWNING IS great for relieving stress and enhancing relaxation. When you yawn, the body receives a burst of oxygen that helps energize and relax you. So don't stifle your yawns!

IF YOUR mind is overactive at bedtime, try this hydrotherapy treatment. Soak a pair of cotton socks in cold water, wring out and put them on the feet. Put another pair of dry cotton socks over the top. The cool temperature will draw the blood away from the head and help calm the brain.

AVOID EATING late at night if you suffer from sleep-related problems. Although you might feel drowsy after a large meal, when you sleep your body's metabolism and digestive activity slows down, which can lead to a disturbed night's sleep.

TRY TO go to bed and get up at the same time each day.

unwind

relax

recharge

chill out

revive

replenish

revitalize

learn to relax

If you lead a stressful lifestyle, it is important to learn to switch off at the end of a busy day with therapies or practices that can easily be incorporated into your lifestyle. Never use lack of time as an excuse to keep you from meditating, doing yoga, or performing stretching exercises. *Make* the time.

One of the most effective ways to manage stress is through the age-old practice of meditation. It focuses your thoughts and is a great way to calm your mind and body, release your troubles, and expel toxins from the body. There are many different meditation techniques, some of which are best taught by an expert. However, you might want to incorporate the following simple meditation technique into your daily life.

Retreat to a quiet place, away from all interruptions. Sit up comfortably straight in a chair, with your feet flat on the floor. Place your hands on your knees with the palms facing the ceiling. Close your eyes and slow your breathing: breathe in through your nose, counting to 10, and out through your mouth, counting to six. Repeat several times until you feel relaxed. Then channel your thoughts to an object of your choice—an imaginary flower, say. As you drift into a deeply relaxed state, continue to picture this object. If your mind starts to wander, refocus. Try to remain in this state for 10 minutes. Sit quietly for several minutes before getting up. Practice this technique twice a day, or whenever you feel under pressure.

relaxation techniques

yoga routine

Yoga, meaning "yoke," unites the mind and body through exercise, breathing and meditation. When you are in a relaxed state, the oxygen level in your bloodstream is higher and the body is in balance. Yoga, whether it is a passive form (such as hatha yoga), or a more dynamic form (such as power yoga, or ashtanga vinyasa yoga), has the ability to tone the body and improve flexibility. Through different controlled movements you stretch, bend, and twist, breathe more deeply, energize the body, release trapped nerves, and expand your muscles. The various yoga postures are known as asanas.

To master yoga it is advisable to attend classes. Your instructor will be able to advise you on different moves and techniques to practice at home. Once you have perfected the moves, practice yoga daily to clear your mind and relieve tension in your body.

stretching

Stretching postures act like an internal massage for the body. Combined with breathing exercises, they can totally reenergize the body. Start off with this basic stretching technique: Stand up straight, with your feet shoulder-width apart, and stretch your arms straight out in front of you. Gently lean over and try (without forcing the movement) to touch your toes. Uncurl and stretch up. Repeat this movement 10 to 15 times. Shake your arms and legs and gently roll your head around from left to right. Consider attending a gym and doing stretching classes; when you become agile and know what you are doing, you can practice the stretches at home. Do not stretch if your muscles are not warm. Either jog in place for a short while, or take a warm shower, before doing any stretching exercises. You should not experience pain while stretching, so never force it.

relaxation techniques

t'ai chi

Known as "meditation in motion," t'ai chi is an ancient Chinese martial art that combines meditation and exercise to promote total well-being. It has been proved that regular practice of t'ai chi relaxes and de-stresses the muscles and nervous system. This, in turn, benefits the glandular system, boosts metabolism, and enhances the power of the immune system. It also improves posture, flexibility, and circulation.

T'ai chi involves following a series of slow, flowing movements: 24 of them in the shorter sequence, which takes from 5 to 10 minutes to complete, and 108 in the longer sequence, which takes between 40 and 60 minutes. These movements help balance the flow of chi (energy) within the body. In China it is traditional to practice t'ai chi outdoors, especially in wooded areas, in order to absorb the energy emitted by trees. To find a qualified t'ai chi instructor, consult your local alternative health association.

muscular relaxation

Progressive Muscular Relaxation (PMR) is a physical technique used to relieve tense muscles and to relax the body. This relaxation technique works on the basis of tensing a group of muscles, holding them in their contracted state for a few seconds, releasing them and then relaxing them further. Perform PMR techniques at your desk, on the train, or in the bath. For head-to-toe relaxation, start with the muscles in the feet and then work up the body, contracting different muscle groups. When you release each group of muscles, imagine you are releasing all your worries and tension. When the pressure is on, clench your fists as tightly as possible, hold them for several seconds, release, and then completely relax the muscles. It instantly relieves anger and anxiety. To increase the benefits of PMR, focus on your breathing. Try inhaling deeply through your nose while tensing your muscles, and exhale through your mouth as you release your muscles.

relaxation techniques

breathing exercises

When we breathe we usually exhale only about one tenth of the air that is in our lungs. The oxygen-rich air we inhale has to mix with the stale, carbon dioxide-laden air that remains in our lungs. When we are stressed we are often tense, especially in the jaw, chest, and diaphragm, and we take very shallow breaths. This means that the amount of oxygen in our bloodstream is reduced, impairing our ability to think clearly and feel relaxed.

To enhance your breathing ability, incorporate this simple exercise into your daily routine. Sit in a chair with your chin parallel to the floor. Inhale slowly through the nose, filling your abdomen and chest completely. Breathe out through your mouth to expel all the oxygen from your lungs. Breathe in deeply again through the nose, lifting your torso muscles to fill your body with air, then breathe out slowly through the mouth. Repeat several times until you feel relaxed and revitalized.

positive thinking

When you are under pressure, try to be aware of your thoughts. Normally, if we have negative thoughts—such as worrying about what other people think of us—these thoughts come and go without affecting us unduly. However, when we are under pressure, our anxieties can become magnified. It is advisable, therefore, to become aware of the thoughts going through your head. Write them down and review them rationally. Often your anxieties will not have any basis in reality or can be solved in an instant. By addressing them early, they should not become recurring worries. To help overcome negative thoughts and feelings of insecurity, devise a personal mantra (literally, a phrase or word describing what you mean to do and be). When stressed, repeat this mantra in your head. It could be a phrase like, "I can do this" or "I am in control of my life." Use your mantra to overcome difficulties and remain in control.

relaxation techniques

aromatherapy

Using pure essential oils extracted from plants can help reduce both physical and emotional stresses. It takes just 2 seconds for an aroma to enter the nose and travel to the part of the brain that stores memories and controls emotions. Some odoriferous molecules actually penetrate the skin to take action, while others stimulate nerve endings as they are inhaled. With the exception of lavender and tea tree oil, neat essential oils should not be applied directly to the skin. Blend with a carrier or base oil, such as jojoba or sweet almond oil. Use a ratio of nine drops of essential oil to 1 oz (30 ml) of carrier oil. To relieve stress, try a mixture of lavender, rose, and chamomile. To boost a flagging spirit, try ylang-ylang and neroli.

aromatherapy guidelines

Store essential oils and oil blends in airtight, dark glass bottles. Shake before use. If doing a massage, warm the oil in your hands beforehand. Oil blends can be added directly to the bath. Never have an aromatherapy massage and then take a bath—you will wash away the skin-conditioning benefits of the oils. Once oils have been absorbed into the body via the skin, their effects remain true from 4 to 6 hours, provided you don't drink alcohol or caffeine in that time. If you are pregnant, suffer from high blood pressure, epilepsy, or any other medical condition, avoid aromatherapy oils unless you consult a qualified aromatherapist or doctor. Buy reputable brands of essential oils—price is often a good indication of quality.

soothing massage

the benefits

Massage is medically proven to reduce levels of stress hormones and release the body's natural feel-good hormones (called endorphins). Book yourself a professional massage or learn how to do self-massage. Use aromatherapy oils to double the benefits.

body work

For head-to-toe stress relief, give yourself a full-body massage. Start with the soles of the feet, then sweep your hands over the ankles and up the legs. Massage your stomach, breast, and décolleté next, then your arms and face (see page 65 for facial massage instructions). To ease tight shoulders and knots in the neck, glide your hands over the area with sweeping motions and then knead your knuckles into the area. Finish by rolling your head gently from left to right.

head massage

To relieve a tight scalp and headache, treat yourself to an invigorating head massage. Start by gently running your fingers through your hair, working from the forehead over the crown and down to the nape of your neck. Repeat this motion several times to relax yourself. Then, using the pads of the fingertips, make small, circular motions over the scalp, working from the forehead to the back of your neck. Focus on the areas around the ears and at the base of the neck, as these are places where tension has a tendency to build up. Finally, place the hands on either side of the head, with the fingers covering the ears and the heels of your hands by the temples, and exert gentle pressure for a few seconds. Slowly release the pressure and glide your hands up to the top of your head. Repeat this motion several times.

instant relaxation

FILL YOUR room with a relaxing aroma. Try burning sandalwood incense, or vapourizing lavender, chamomile, and ylang-ylang essential oils.

TAKE A warm bath laced with five drops of lavender oil. Lavender is reputed to relieve aches and pains and soothe the nervous system.

KISS YOUR partner. When you have a passionate embrace with a loved one, the body releases a flood of feel-good hormones.

RELEASE ALL your tension and frustrations by shouting. The louder you shout, the better you'll feel.

CLOSE YOUR eyes and massage your temples with the pads of your fingers, working in small, circular motions.

SPEND TIME with a pet. Research has shown that caring for an animal, and enjoying the companionship they provide, is one of the best antidotes to stress.

LISTEN TO music that evokes fond memories of a special time, place, person, or event.

INVEST IN a mini-trampoline and spend 10 minutes on it each day. In addition to boosting circulation and enhancing cardiovascular activity, it relieves tension and brings some fun to your day.

relax

unwind

indulge

pampering treats

enjoy

treat

gratify

how does stress affect our looks?

Premature aging, hair loss, dull complexions, blemishes, and skin problems like eczema can all occur as a result of stress. When the pressure is on, free-radical activity speeds up within the body. Free radicals are rogue molecules that are largely the by-product of oxidation (the same process that causes cars to rust). A certain amount of free-radical activity is needed to kill bacteria and germs, but problems arise when the body produces too many free radicals and the process gets out of control. Each healthy cell is likely to receive 10,000 damaging "hits" from free radicals every day. Accumulated damage to cells paves the way to premature aging and hair loss. Research has shown that free-radical activity is also in part responsible for at least 50 of our most common diseases.

Taking time out from the stresses of life will slow the attack on your cells, making you look younger and feel healthier for longer. Do your body a favor and treat yourself to a facial or a massage … Indulge in an aromatherapy bath … Or take a tip from Zen culture and spend some time alone in reflection. This is known as "cultivating emptiness," and it helps to clear the mind and remove stress from your life.

hair-care regimen

hair problems

Female hair loss or thinning has increased dramatically over the past 20 years. In most cases the loss is only temporary and is the result of a particularly stressful situation, or it occurs postpregnancy when hormone levels and vital nutrients drop dramatically. Hair loss is caused by lack of oxygen. The cells that form and support the hair follicle stop dividing and eventually die. This results in the hair follicle collapsing inward, halting new hair growth. Highly alkaline shampoos, silicone-based hair products, and insufficient rinsing can lead to buildups on the scalp, accelerating asphyxiation.

Other hair problems are caused by heavy waxes and gels, which adhere to the scalp, block follicles, and lead to sebaceous cysts and bacterial irritation. Find alternative, healthier hair products.

scalp care

Treat the scalp to regular massages to promote healthy hair growth and relieve tension. Use warm olive oil to massage and treat the scalp. Massage with the pads of the fingers and work in small circular motions, exerting gentle pressure. Start above the forehead and work toward the crown and down to the nape of the neck. Leave the oil on, preferably overnight (use a towel to protect your pillowcase), to treat a scalp that may be dry and flaky as a result of stress. To wash out, apply shampoo to dry hair and then wash as usual. Brush your hair regularly to help maintain scalp condition. If your brush or comb has broken bristles or teeth, throw it away, otherwise it could scratch the scalp. If your scalp feels tight when you're tense, tip your head upside down and run your fingertips over the scalp.

stress-ease solutions

skin disorders

Emotional stress is attributed to many skin complaints, including psoriasis, eczema, acne, and rosacea. When the pressure is on, the immune system's white blood cells cling to the blood vessels' walls. This creates redness, sensitivity, and irritation and leads to skin disorders. Try to reduce the stress in your life to see your skin improve.

pace yourself

Experts maintain that it is more important to wash our feet than our faces; feet excrete many toxins. Fill a large bowl with warm water and add a couple of drops of lavender oil. Place your feet in the bowl and gently flex them, contracting and relaxing the muscles. After 10 minutes, dry your feet and massage them with skin cream.

soak it up

For a relaxing bath, try adding two drops each of rose, chamomile, cedarwood, and sandalwood oil to the bath water, or simply add five drops of lavender oil. After bathing, if you plan to go to bed, pat the skin dry and then massage the soles of the feet with coconut oil to help instill a sense of peace and harmony.

premature aging

Stress can accelerate the aging process. To help maintain a healthy complexion, avoid the sun (or wear a high-SPF sunscreen when exposed to the sun), make sure you follow a nutritious, balanced eating regimen, drink plenty of water, get enough sleep, and follow an effective skincare regimen.

indulge yourself

stressed skin

When we are unhappy and feeling stressed, the chances are we won't be looking our best. Often, when we are stressed, the skin's oil-producing glands go into overdrive and skin can become excessively oily and prone to blemishes. Treat by dabbing neat tea tree oil onto the area.

skin illumination

Stress often plays havoc with skin condition, so if your complexion looks dull and lifeless, try a deep-cleansing treatment. Fill a bowl with boiling water, place a towel over your head, and hold your head about 4 in (10 cm) away from the surface of the water. Steam for 5 minutes, then slather on a deep-cleansing face mask. Clay masks are good for purifying the skin, since they contain active ingredients that absorb impurities. Be sure the skin's moisture levels are restored after cleansing. Avoid deep-cleansing treatments if you have sensitive skin.

face value

Give yourself a boost with a facial massage. Use moisturizer or an aromatherapy blend. For normal/dry complexions, blend $1/3$ oz (10 ml) of jojoba or sweet almond oil with three drops of rose oil, and for normal/oily complexions mix with three drops of geranium oil. Using both hands, massage up from the middle of the forehead and along the hairline. Apply gentle pressure on the temples. Repeat this action three times, then sweep the hands around the eyes and lightly tap the surrounding skin. Exert gentle pressure on the point between the eyes for a few seconds. Glide your hands over the cheeks, applying pressure as you work along the contours. Sweep the fingers around the nose and under the cheekbones. Stroke both sides of the nose and then exert gentle pressure around the base of the nose. Press the central point on the upper lip and then encircle the mouth. Finally, sweep the hands down over the chin and neck.

look good, feel good

RETREAT TO your bathroom or bedroom and spend the evening pampering yourself. Give yourself a facial, manicure, and pedicure—you'll feel relaxed and look great.

FEELING ANXIOUS? Lie down and place two cold chamomile tea bags on your eyes. This will calm you and help treat the delicate skin around the eyes.

IF YOU have problems sleeping, place a drop of lavender oil on your pillow. It should help you relax.

SLATHER ON a face mask. Not only will it condition the skin, it will give you time to relax and unwind.

WHEN APPLYING hand cream, give yourself an express massage. Clasp your hands together and rotate each wrist in turn, then continue to work the cream into the skin.

SPLASH WATER on your face whenever you're feeling out of control. Cold water steps up circulation, making you feel invigorated.

EAT CHOCOLATE: It contains theobromine and phenylethlamine, antidepressants that are believed to trigger the release of neurochemicals that give us a natural high. Remember, though, that chocolate affects blood sugar levels, so eat it in moderation.

contentment

acceptance

calm

de-stress solutions

peace

harmony

balance

de-stress solutions

laughing matter

Laughing helps relieve anxiety, depression, and pain; it triggers the release of endorphins from the brain. Laughing also helps fight infection by raising levels of immunoglobin A in the blood, which boosts the activity of the white blood cells. When we smile, all the major facial muscles are made to relax. This sets off an emotional reaction that makes us feel good.

stop smoking

Though the short-term effects of nicotine can be to make one feel more relaxed, nicotine in fact raises the heart rate and stresses the body. If you smoke, try taking your pulse rate before and after smoking a cigarette, and notice the difference. To ease the withdrawal symptoms of quitting, take a vitamin B supplement. If, after giving up, you have a craving, stimulate the acupressure point by gently squeezing the tip of the thumb and exerting gentle pressure for 60 seconds.

work environment

Feeling anxious about work? Before you start the day, try vaporizing geranium oil in an oil burner. Geranium is reputed to instill peace. If you are having difficulty concentrating, inhale rosemary, and if you are feeling tired by midafternoon, burn some energizing peppermint oil.

nurturing solution

Breastfeeding is a great antidote to stress. Mothers who breastfeed are more likely to have high levels of oxytocin—a hormone that soothes areas of the brain involved in emotions and stress—after feeding their babies. They also have lower blood pressure readings after a stressful event.

chew it

A dry mouth can often be a sign of stress. Try chewing gum—it will stimulate the salivary glands and help to moisten the mouth. Just don't let chewing gum become a habit, because it can lead to dental problems.

de-stress solutions

herbal high

Saint-John's-wort, or hypericum, is said to lift flagging spirits, treat depression, and alleviate seasonal affective disorder. Its primary ingredient, hypericin, is believed to enhance the action of the brain's soothing neurotransmitters. Kava kava, an herbal extract made from the Pacific Islands pepper plant, works to banish stress in a different way. It is believed to block the production of the brain's anxiety-producing neurotransmitter. Take Saint-John's-wort and kava kava only on the advice of a medical practitioner. They can have harmful side effects, and correct dosage is vital.

food force

If you lead a stressful lifestyle, increase your intake of foods rich in vitamin C. The adrenal glands (those that produce adrenaline) use vitamin C when the body is experiencing physical stress. Eat plenty of fresh fruits and vegetables to ensure that your reserves of this vitamin are high.

new brew

If you have around four cups of average-strength coffee a day, or six cups of black tea, there's a good chance you may be caffeine dependent. Studies have revealed that people who consume four cups of coffee every day have higher levels of the stress hormone epinephrine in their bodies than noncaffeine drinkers (on the average, 30 percent more). They also tend to have higher blood pressure. To reduce this bodily stress, cut down on your intake of caffeine and increase your intake of fresh juice, water, and herbal tea.

get physical

Exercise instantly relieves stress. It encourages good blood flow, ensuring that vital oxygen and nutrients are transported around the body. Experts recommend 30 minutes of moderate exercise every day. Even short bursts of activity adding up to this amount of time are enough to keep us healthy.

de-stress solutions

be happy
Look on the bright side of life. Studies have revealed that there are strong links between our state of mind and the effectiveness of our immune system. Being happy enhances our immune responses and makes us better able to deal with stressful situations.

culinary advice
When the pressure is on, don't force yourself to eat if you're not hungry. Instead of eating a large meal, opt for a juice or some soup—meals that are gentler on the digestive system. When you have de-stressed, eat a healthy, nutritious meal.

stomach settler
If you suffer from a nervous stomach when under pressure, avoid white wine, cheese, tomatoes, vinegar, and refined sugar products. To quell feelings of anxiety in the stomach, either drink a glass of milk before a meal or sip a cup of chamomile tea.

spicy vice
If you're stressed-out and feeling at a low ebb, try eating hot, spicy foods. When you eat chillies, for example, the nerves sense pain and tell the brain to release endorphins.

tension release
Having fun helps relieve tension. Stressed-out people are less likely to participate in fun activities than those who are more relaxed.

foot work
There are thousands of nerve endings on the soles of the feet, and these correspond to all the major organs in the body. Rub the feet and literally knead the soles using your knuckles. If you have tension in your left shoulder, massage your left foot and vice versa; apply pressure between each toe and hold each toe firmly. If you suffer from tension in the shoulders, try rubbing the underside of your little toe on the outside of each foot.

de-stress solutions

calming essences

Inhaling certain aromas will stimulate the production of the brain's relaxing chemical, serotonin. Apply a few drops of either lavender or chamomile oil to a cotton handkerchief, place over the nose and inhale deeply.

pressure zone

Often anxiety can result in tense jaw muscles. To relieve the tension, simply press your tongue on the roof of your mouth behind the teeth. To ease a headache, massage the tips of your big toes, exerting gentle pressure.

imagine it

Visualization is a great stress reliever. When you are at a low ebb, close your eyes, and envisage your favorite place. Imagine the sounds and smells that go with the picture in your mind, and escape into that place.

relaxing treat

If you're feeling stressed, soak a washcloth in a bowl of warm water with three drops of lavender essential oil added. Wring out the cloth, lie down, and place the cloth on your forehead. Breathe deeply and relax.

water works

When you're feeling anxious, sip a glass of warm water. Drinking warm water has much more of a calming effect than cold water. To help relieve tension, try floating in a swimming pool, floatation tank, or even in the bathtub.

pace work

To relieve stress, take your shoes off and walk on wet grass or sand. This will massage your feet and help relieve bodily and mental tension. Moreover, it will strengthen your toes for general foot conditioning.

Published by Time-Life Books, a division of Time Life Inc.
Time-Life is a trademark of Time Warner Inc. and affiliated companies.

Time-Life Books
Vice President and Publisher: Neil S. Levin
Vice President, Content Development: Jennifer L. Pearce
Senior Sales Director: Richard J. Vreeland
Director, Marketing and Publicity: Inger Forland
Director of New Product Development: Carolyn M. Clark
Director of Custom Publishing: John Lalor
Director of Rights and Licensing: Olga Vezeris
Executive Editor: Linda Bellamy
Director of Design: Tina Taylor

First published in 2000 by Murdoch Books®,
a division of Murdoch Magazines Pty Ltd,
GPO Box 1203, Sydney, NSW Australia 2001

Photographer: Chris Craymer
Creative Director/Stylist: Jane Campsie
Concept & Design: Marylouise Brammer
Project Manager: Anna Waddington
Editor: Susan Gray
Hair Stylist: Martyn Gayle
Make-up Artist: Attracta Courtney
Models: India Bluett, Greg Butler, Ceri Evans, Molly Hallam, Sarah Hannon,
Lindi Hingston, Irmina, Kirsty Lee Axford, Trese San-Wong
Shoot Production: Susie Bluett at Susie Bluett Productions

Group General Manager: Mark Smith
Publisher: Kay Scarlett
Production Manager: Liz Fitzgerald

Library of Congress Cataloging-in-Publication Data available upon request.
ISBN 0-7370-3024-0

Printed by Toppan Printing Hong Kong Co. Ltd.
PRINTED IN CHINA. This edition printed 2001.